When *Shift* Happens

21 DAYS OF CELEBRATING THE LESSONS OF LIFE & DETOURS

Charron Monaye

When Shifts Happen: 21 Days of Celebrating the Lessons of Life and Detours©
Written By: Charron Monaye, 2020

ALL RIGHTS RESERVED. No part of this book may be reproduced in any written, electronic, recording, or photocopying without written permission of the publisher or author. The exception would be in the case of brief quotations embodied in the critical articles or reviews and pages where permission is specifically granted by the publisher or author.

Published By: Pen Legacy®
Cover By: Christian Cuan
Editing & Formatting By:
Carla M. Dean of U Can Mark My Word

Library of Congress Cataloging–in-Publication Data has been applied for.

ISBN: 978-1734827-87-3

PRINTED IN THE UNITED STATES OF AMERICA

.

Dedication

This book is dedicated to my sons, Christopher and Craig. Do not get weary or lose sight of the goal when shifts happen within your life. Learn from them. Use the message as your instructional guide on how to proceed. Life is full of trials and challenges, but it's not the shift that defines you. It's how you respond to it. This book will offer my perspective on things to consider as you journey throughout this life. I hope that after completing this book, your response will make every trial possible, and greatness will flow from it.

21/90 Rule

It takes **21 *days*** to make a ***Habit*** and ***90 days*** to make a ***Lifestyle***.

Are You Ready?

TABLE OF CONTENTS

I Bet You Didn't See It Coming	11

Part I The Work

Change Your Mind, Change Your Life	21
Expect Nothing	31

Part II 21 Days of Celebrating the Shift

Prayer for Gratitude	43
Day 1: I Celebrate Myself	45
Day 2: I Celebrate My Mistakes	51
Day 3: I Celebrate My Heartbreak	57
Day 4: I Celebrate My Divorce	63
Day 5: I Celebrate My Childhood	69
Day 6: I Celebrate My Choices	75
Day 7: I Celebrate My Relationships	81
Day 8: I Celebrate My Faith	87
Day 9: I Celebrate My Vision	93
Day 10: I Celebrate My Finances	99
Day 11: I Celebrate My Intention	105
Day 12: I Celebrate My Love	111
Day 13: I Celebrate My Enemies	117
Day 14: I Celebrate My Job, Career, or Work	123
Day 15: I Celebrate My Marriage	129

Day 16: I Celebrate My Failures	133
Day 17: I Celebrate My Life	139
Day 18: I Celebrate My Ability to Relocate	145
Day 19: I Celebrate Change	151
Day 20: I Forgive Myself Letter	157
Day 21: Permission Slip of Life	161
Acknowledgements	167
About The Author	171

When *Shift* Happens

21 DAYS OF CELEBRATING THE LESSONS OF LIFE & DETOURS

I Bet You Didn't See It Coming

It was June 3, 2014, and the kids and I had just pulled in front of the house. Right when we got out of the car to go inside, I received a call.

"I just spoke to your brother," the caller said. "He said it's not safe for you to live there, and you need to move before the end of the month."

Those words changed my life. Where would I go? Having moved only six months prior, I did not foresee being evicted by my brother, especially since my rent was current and paid. That phone call damaged my ability to trust and made it easy for me to believe that the saying "blood is no thicker than water" was true. But, like always, my God showed up right on time, and another family member offered me a place to stay for as long as I needed. I promised myself then that if God protected my sons and me, I would never allow another man to disappoint me again.

Once I got us settled in our new home, I immediately went into shifting my life. From my mindset to my finances, I did a complete overhaul of who Charron was and what she would accept from people. I developed grudges and created boundaries to prevent anyone from throwing another curveball that could affect my children and me. I kept my distance from most everyone. Putting my faith and trust in God, I prayed to him for guidance on how to clean up the mess that I was handed. To this day, I still can't tell you how my life was uprooted when I thought I was doing everything right. What I have learned is that when shifts happen, very seldom do they have anything to do with us directly. Shifts are more so to show us where we are losing focus or unprepared. I can admit that back then, I was blindsided. However, when you get laser-focused on believing that you are the only person you can trust, you begin to look at life differently, and with a readiness mindset, you start taking ownership of your life.

After avoiding being homeless and rebuilding my life after divorce, you would have thought that I would have been better prepared when faced with another financial meltdown. Nope! Even though I did not see it coming, I was faced with the struggle to rebuild my life yet again. For years, I blamed myself for not learning from the mistakes I had made in my marriage, but once again, I found myself vulnerable—my life disrupted by others. I always tell people that it's one thing if I decide to destroy my life, but it's something horrific when others cause harm to me with no regard. My marriage did a mental beating on me; however, the situation concerning my brother left not only a stain on my heart but a permanent resolve never to have to depend on others. This shift made me promise to myself to get ahead in life so that I would never again find myself placed in a position where being blindsided could cost me. That situation and the revelation it provided caused the paradigm shift that created the woman you see today.

How do you respond when life abruptly changes? Aside from trying to cope with today's COVID-19 pandemic, how many of you have faced a life-altering situation that blindsided you, leaving you confused on how to regroup? How did you handle the situation you didn't see coming while remaining focused on living? Life has a funny way of throwing you curveballs and leaving you to figure out how to dodge the blows. Many of us have yet to master ducking while walking through life, while others understand that to win life's battles, you need faith, focus, and a great catch. I have been faced with and overcame a divorce, legal judgments, insecurities, heartbreak, financial instabilities, and unemployment throughout my journey. I was forced to repeat the pain of some of these situations simply because I did not receive the full lesson the first time. Once I got tired of losing, I created the ***Prayer, Manifest, Plan, Prepare,*** and ***Celebrate*** formula. I became clear on what I wanted, why it was important to me, who could assist me in getting what I wanted, and how to implement my plan. I started embracing the mantra, *"See the glass half full, never half empty."*

Don't get me wrong. Repositioning myself from a place of merely existing in life to living with purpose and peace was not as easy as I am going to make it seem in this book. When raised with a lack of optimism, you have to retrain your mind to think that every negative thing has a positive purpose attached. In addition to shifting my mindset to see the glass as half full instead of half empty, I gained a sense of readiness to get ahead of life's situations. This way, when life did occur, I permitted myself to see the blessing that lies ahead instead of focusing on the issue at hand because I was already prepared for it. The peace that came from this shift was truly rewarding. Plus, it kept my anxiety down. Can we say #winning?

In this book, I will help you to see life's challenges as blessings instead of blockages. Everything you have endured thus far happened for a reason. Have you ever lost a job, and rather than wallowing in your pity with you, people encouraged you by saying God had something better for you or reminded you that when one door closes, another opens? That is the optimistic mindset I am challenging you to have as you go through these 21 days. To assist you, I coach you through daily conversations to change your perspective on a particular situation. Also, I provide prayers of gratitude and journaling prompts to transform your mindset from seeing things as being half-empty to half-full. While you work towards completing this 21-day process, it is my goal to help you recognize the good in every situation, even if it had the ability to break you. Faith and worry cannot co-exist in the same mind. So, we have to get clear on the emotion that we give most of our power and focus on faith instead of fear.

Throughout my life's experience, I have learned it is not what happens to you that defines you but how you respond. Until 2014, I had a very optimistic outlook regarding situations in my life; however, I kept living without learning the lesson to prevent certain things from happening again. For instance, my divorce should have broken me, but instead, I lived like I would be blessed with true love one day soon. Facing a housing court judge should have belittled me, but I lived like my finances would get better. When I lost my job, I simply updated my resume, confident that someone would ultimately hire me. Even though periods of loss should have destroyed me, I lived as if tomorrow was a new day to get it right and come out on top. I had many chances to respond differently to the shifts that offered me a new way of living, but instead of learning from the experiences, I ignored the lessons because I was too busy to sit still.

As you know, life does not slow down or stop when we have a problem. I don't know about you, but to me, it seems to move faster. As a mother, employee, and entrepreneur, I didn't have time to analyze my experiences to truly understand what went wrong and how I could do better. I mean, who has time to self-reflect these days? For me, self-reflecting was unheard of. That is until 2014, when life decided to knock me down. It's funny how life gets our attention when we think we have it all figured out. Little did I know, I had much more to learn, and my learning started when I had to move but had nowhere to go.

As much as I blamed others for the horrible situation I found myself in, I eventually owned my part and shifted the blame from them to me. No matter what life threw my way, I should have never been unprepared. If I had been prepared, that shift wouldn't have broken me. However, since life has a way of shifting our perspective and perception, it was necessary to save my life and celebrate the circumstances, looking at them with a winning attitude instead of panicking. I can honestly say I am forever indebted to 2014 because that year created the execution of my desires and my ability to experience them now. Everything I prayed for and did the work to receive, I now own—from relocating to Wesley Chapel, Florida, from Philadelphia, living near a lake, having an emergency fund, having a back-up plan, receiving a promotion at work, and having a profitable business. My glass is not just half-full; it's full.

Today, I am focused on celebrating life rather than just living in it! My shift awarded me with purpose, and that is what I hope for you by the time you finish this book. It is time to take a seat, be still, and honestly analyze your experiences to get clear on what the lessons are trying to rescue you from encountering. I pray for your success as you embark on your new celebration of life.

Part I

The Work

Change Your Mind, Change Your Life

Before we go any further, can we agree that your mindset is one hundred percent the blame for you making certain choices, remaining in situations that no longer serve you, and accepting things that don't help elevate you? What you have told yourself through the years has either brainwashed you into thinking life is supposed to be this way, or it motivates you to achieve more because you know you deserve it. Your mind is the vessel that controls your actions by embedding the very attitudes, attributes, emotions, values, and feelings you express through life. For example, when something happens that you don't like, your first instinct is to respond emotionally based on your thoughts and feelings. Some people react with an attitude and become defensive; others will back away so as not to elevate the drama, and a few will choose to ignore or handle their displeasure silently. Regardless of how you decide to attack a situation, to achieve a better result, we must understand how to change the way we think.

To understand how to change your mindset, we must first examine the two types of mindsets: fixed and growth.

- **Fixed Mindset.** People with a fixed mindset believe their qualities are inborn, fixed, and unchangeable.
- **Growth Mindset.** People who have a growth mindset believe their abilities can be developed and strengthened by way of commitment and hard work.

As you can see, the biggest difference between the two types of mindsets is how you view your ability to grow. Sometimes our mindset is created by our parents projecting their beliefs and fears onto us, but we have the power to adjust our lives to fit our thoughts, needs, and desires. For example, have you ever seen a child who was extremely concerned with being judged or feared they might not live up to their parents' expectations? The pressure alone could have the child thinking they have no control over their life or that nothing they ever do is good enough. Can anyone relate? How many of you are more concerned with others' expectations than your own happiness? This kind of mindset, if not adjusted, will lead a person down a negative path because of the emotions and feelings it evokes.

With a fixed mindset, the person always needs validation. When you feel like you're being judged, you tend to live a life trying to please everyone and often end up heartbroken. Again, who am I speaking to? Are you that person? I am also guilty of being a people pleaser. In my book, *Stop Asking for Permission and Give Notice*, I speak about my journey of overcoming being a people pleaser and how I lived for the approval of others. Their approval validated my success and determined whether I would continue or cease whatever I was doing. Let me tell you, that was an exhausting life. Half the time, I did not even know who I was; I was just going with the flow while dying on the inside.

However, as I regained control of my life, I developed more into a growth mindset. It was in this mindset where I found the power and peace to accept my need for personal growth, happiness, freedom, and love. I became clear about what I wanted, and I took proactive steps to receive it. I started exploring new things and people by networking with those who were outside of my comfort zone. I embraced new experiences and enjoyed challenges to grow beyond what I once thought was impossible. I started seeing mistakes as learning lessons and stopped at nothing to correct them in a way that would be most beneficial for me. As my belief in myself changed, so did my life. It was like I became unstoppable, and everything I once prayed for finally started coming true.

So, as you see, it wasn't until I owned my life that I could grow my mindset to create the life I wanted. Ask yourself, do you own your life, or are you renting space and settling for less? To relieve stress and celebrate life, you must understand your mindset. How you think and what you believe is not only affecting your results, but it costs you freedom, as well. To help you understand your mindset, I have created a list of statements with which you will either agree or disagree. Your response will gain you a better understanding of how you think. Can you guess which statements are based on a fixed mindset and which are of a growth mindset?

1. You try to hide your flaws to avoid being judged or labeled a failure.
2. Your flaws are a TO-DO list of things for you to improve.

3. You stick with doing what you know to keep up your confidence.
4. You keep up your confidence by always pushing into the unfamiliar, ensuring you're continuously learning and expanding your mind.
5. You commit to mastering valuable skills regardless of your mood, knowing that passion and purpose come from doing great work, which comes from expertise and experience.
6. Failures define you.
7. Failures are temporary setbacks.
8. You believe if you're romantically compatible with someone, you should share all of each other's views, and everything should just come naturally.
9. You believe a lasting relationship comes from effort and working through inevitable differences.
10. It's about the outcome. If you fail, you think it was all wasted time and effort.
11. It's about the process, so the outcome hardly matters.

So how did you do? Following are the statements with the answer to the kind of mindset they are:

1. You try to hide your flaws to avoid being judged or labeled a failure. *(Fixed)*
2. Your flaws are a TO-DO list of things for you to improve. *(Growth)*
3. You stick with doing what you know to keep up your confidence. *(Fixed)*
4. You keep up your confidence by always pushing into the unfamiliar, ensuring you're continuously learning and expanding your mind. *(Growth)*
5. You commit to mastering valuable skills regardless of your mood, knowing that passion and purpose come from doing great work, which comes from expertise and experience. *(Growth)*
6. Failures define you. *(Fixed)*
7. Failures are temporary setbacks. *(Growth)*
8. You believe if you're romantically compatible with someone, you should share all of each other's views, and everything should just come naturally. *(Fixed)*
9. You believe a lasting relationship comes from effort and working through inevitable differences. *(Growth)*
10. It's about the outcome. If you fail, you think it was all wasted time and effort. (Fixed)
11. It's about the process, so the outcome hardly matters. *(Growth)*

What kind of mindset do you have? Fixed, growth, or a mixture of both? Being clear on how you think will help as you go through this book and as you journey through life. Having a growth mindset is the key that separates winners from losers or struggling entrepreneurs from mogul millionaires. How hard are you willing to fight for what you want? Do you see your competitor as an adversary or a potential partner? Do you believe you are worthy of what you ask to receive?

When you change your mindset, you change your life. I am profoundly grateful that I was able to change from a mentality of settling to having a mindset of achieving what others may view as impossible. I took all the sticks, stones, and heartbreaks thrown at me and created a queendom that now rewards me. Are you ready to transition from fixed to growth? Are you prepared to watch the universe manifest it for you? Here are seven things I did to develop a growth mindset while transforming my life:

1. Be willing to learn something daily.
2. Understand that perseverance is key.
3. Embrace challenges.
4. Develop a sense of personal responsibility.
5. Appreciate failure.
6. Accept constructive criticism.
7. Celebrate others with no motive.

Charron Monaye

Not until you shift your mindset to accept life for what it is will you begin to see that it's not the end of the world when shifts happen. Sometimes shifts occur to change the narrative or give us an advantage. Stop looking at the glass as half full and see it as always full because you now have something of value to add to it. You are responsible for your life. No matter the disruption or the damage along your path, you are given another chance to get it right every day when you wake up. It is time for you to commit to a new life—a life that is devoted to who you are and who you are becoming.

Author, public speaker, life coach, and philanthropist Tony Robbins once said, "If you want lasting change, you've got to give up this idea of 'trying something.' You've got to decide you're going to commit-to-mastery." It's time to quit "trying" and just go for it. As I stated before, it's not easy. It took me multiple lessons before I got it right, but now, I am living according to my own rules. Changing my mindset changed my way of thinking and the energy I absorb. It made it easy for me to get out of debt, relocate out of state, accept love that I was unfamiliar with receiving, and end an 18-year connection. The newness that I was able to uncover in four years has been phenomenal.

Are you ready to break every chain? Are you committed to yourself enough to know that you deserve greatness? When you change your mindset, you change your life, and in doing so, it prevents the shifts formed against you from prospering. By creating a growth mindset, you'll be ahead of the storm and will be able to see it before it hits.

Expect Nothing

What are expectations? Besides pressure, expectations are the belief that something we desire will or will not happen. We set expectations when we want to feel that we have complete control over what is to come in our future. For many of us, it is that motivation that drives us to achieve what often looks impossible. It is speaking greatness into the universe and then wanting it to manifest in the physical form. For others, it's that false sense of hope that we tend to lean on when things don't quite look promising, but we create a façade to believe that everything will work out.

If you are anything like myself, you have used expectations to either manifest your good or justify your bad. You expected to win, even though you knew you were not qualified. Moreover, you expected to receive what you wanted simply because you asked for it. But can I offer you something when it comes to expectations? It is perfectly okay to expect everything, but wouldn't life be less stressful and challenging if we removed expectations and allowed ourselves to receive as we aligned ourselves for what we desire? This is a big shift to ask of a person, but it is one that will eliminate much pressure from ourselves.

Stephen Hawking, former Lucasian Professor of Mathematics at the University of Cambridge and author of *A Brief History of Time,* said, "My expectations were reduced to zero when I was 21. Everything since then has been a bonus." Twenty-one is the age Hawking was diagnosed with Lou Gehrig's disease. American poet, novelist, and short-story writer Sylvia Plath once said, "If you expect nothing from anybody, you're never disappointed." Wouldn't life be more rewarding if you allowed it to reward you for your good deeds and work instead of forcing things to happen, only to end up but disappointed when they do not go as you had hoped?

Life, relationships, employers, and friends have all taught me that my expectations have no value. Maybe it's because I can't change how they treat me. Or is it because I had to accept that they would never reciprocate what I offer? At the end of the day, how they treated me was solely based on their perception of me. But who said I had to tolerate it? I am in control of how much unfair treatment I am willing to accept and for how long.

I remember when I had a whole list of things I expected in relationships. I mean, my list was extensive. Guarding my heart was particularly important, and making sure they knew who I was from the gate was mandatory. But, low and behold, every simple thing I expected from my man—loyalty, honesty, patience, love, respect, communication, etc.—were the very things they chose not to give. I expected loyalty; they cheated. I expected honesty; oh chile, could they lie! I expected respect; they caused the tears that would not stop falling. It became a repeat story of my life. My expectations turned into the very things used to hurt me. But why? Did they feel I wasn't worthy of what I asked? Was their perception of me different than who I thought I was? With all my expectations, was I teaching them how to love me through the rules? Was my pressure too much, resulting in eventually driving them to do what I fought so hard to prevent? After analyzing these questions and forgiving myself for allowing it, I destroyed my list of expectations. I promised myself that I would no longer hold anyone to a list of expectations because all it did was leave me divorced and heartbroken.

How could something that you put in place to protect you end up damaging you and make you question your self-worth?

That question ultimately led to me looking at my expectations and how I was applying them to my life. Was I using expectations as rules for others to follow or as a way of protecting myself? Why were my expectations so important? As I did work on myself that consisted of days of soul-searching, I discovered my expectations were never to protect me. It was my way of manipulating others to give me what I wasn't giving myself. I wanted people to validate who I *thought* I was becoming so that I could walk in their acceptance. People were only giving me a reflection of me. They lied to me because oftentimes I lied to myself. They disrespected me because oftentimes I would self-sabotage and talk down to myself. They cheated on me because more often than not, I cheated myself out of things that I knew would help me. My expectations became the mirror of things that I needed to address about myself. How many of you have expected things that eventually blew up in your face because, even though the intent was good, the motive was intended to teach you a lesson? How many of you are expecting something from someone that should be given to you automatically?

As I forced myself to reflect on and change my

ideals of expectations, I had to sit in the truth and get to the root of why. Why did I need to expect anything from anyone? Shouldn't I as a woman, mother, business owner, or employee deserve respect? Asking for respect only gave the person from whom I was making the request permission to treat me how they saw fit. By asking to be respected, it made them aware that I did not believe I was worthy of being respected unless I made the request. However, by voicing my expectations, wouldn't they know without a doubt what is considered acceptable with me? Sometimes, what's not said is enough. Was I doing myself a disservice by expecting? Yes, and my God, did my heart and pocket pay dearly because of it.

After addressing the hard questions and correcting the way I viewed my self-worth, I shifted my mindset from one of expectation to now allowing myself to live freely. At that moment, I took my life back. Instead of having expectations, I allowed people to be who they are, but I set boundaries on how much I was willing to accept. Who people are has nothing to do with you. We go wrong by allowing people to treat us in a way that is not acceptable to us. It has nothing to do with me when my supervisor takes their frustration out on the team. However, when she directs her frustration solely towards me, that's when we have a problem.

My mindset shift has removed much stress and disappointment from my life. Now I am able to hold myself accountable and continue to work on myself when things don't go my way. I learn more effectively from mistakes and can forgive with genuine understanding. I no longer look for validation or confirmation of my self-worth. I know I am worthy of love, so cheating on me is no longer my loss but yours. I am such a great business owner and extremely committed to my calling that instead of expecting God's grace and protection, I trust in His word and know that I already have whatever is meant for me. When you know what you know, you don't have to expect anything. You simply enjoy the journey of receiving it.

We all need this kind of shift to better accept life for what it is. When you take power back from others, you generate a sense of peace and calm that allows you to live with no regrets, disappointments, or heartbreaks. Now do not get me wrong. You will be tried, and people will probably come for you. However, the disappointment from it all will not sting because instead of you expecting more from people, you put yourself first and removed yourself from anything that no longer satisfied you. When you shift the accountability from them to you, you learn how to accept and move on with your dignity, respect, and feelings intact.

When Shift Happens

You are probably thinking, *Charron, this all sounds good, but how did you get to this mindset?* Well, it wasn't easy. Not only did I have to answer the questions I listed above, but I also had to:

- Sit in my truth about who I was
- Accept I will never get me from others
- Get to the bottom of why I needed validation
- Understand how I was showing up for people and situations.

Ultimately, I had to break down my belief system of what I was telling myself. I had to stand in the mirror and speak to my soul while apologizing for allowing people to dictate my feelings, emotions, and movements. When you try to control people with your expectations, they control you with their response. How they react to your rules cannot only have a positive effect by bringing to the surface your flaws to adjust, it can affect your mental and emotional state. Have you ever had someone treat you wrong, and it tears you to pieces? But, instead of you addressing the issues, you blame yourself like only you were to blame. Even if you had very little or nothing to do with it, you find yourself apologizing for something they couldn't handle. Some people will project their issues about your expectations and blame you for setting the bar so high. Don't you hate that? How many of you fall for it?

Then, instead of asking the person if your expectations are too high, you readjust your expectations to meet their inadequateness and are disappointed when they can't deliver. I mean, I would be pissed if I adjusted and lowered my expectations, only for them to play me anyway! This is why the shift is needed.

Why are you upset with them for not being able to live up to your standard, especially when they told you from the start it was too much. Lowering your expectations only gave you a false hope that it would work, when you should have just accepted they're not the one. Hey, everything is not for everyone, and you are not for everybody. By lowering your expectations, you shifted your power, and by them not delivering, you lost hope. Stop putting yourself through this. No expectations! Set boundaries and be okay with knowing that what is for you is for you. You won't have to teach someone how to treat you. You won't have to tolerate so much. You won't have to walk around with so much regret. Remove the expectations and be free just to be. Allow yourself permission to live in your truth and to be who you are. Don't you deserve happiness without placing a list of expectations on it? I would rather not foresee the reward of having someone love me than for me to have to give them directions on how to love me.

Again, your persona and how you show up teaches a person how to treat you. Sure, you can communicate that you like to go on picnics or receive roses now and again, but the basics of how to love, treat, and respect you should not have to be told. How you treat and love yourself will resonate when they speak to you. If you are clear about who you are, they will know what to do without you having to say anything. However, if you show up uncertain, not confident, and looking desperate, nothing you can ever teach them will make them treat you like the queen or king you are.

Part II

21 Days of Celebrating the Shift

Prayer for Gratitude

Dear God,

Thank you for your amazing power and work in my life. Thank you for your goodness and your blessings over me. Thank you for supplying my mind and heart with hope through even the toughest of times, strengthening me for your purposes. Thank you for helping me to see that there are glory and mercy in life's unexpected struggles. That I, too, am a conqueror, and even though weapons will form, they will never prosper. Thank you that you are always with us, even when I refuse to trust your presence. Thank you for never quitting on a sinner like me, for you know my imperfections but never use them against me. Thank you for forgiveness and the ability to call me your child still. Thank you for your incredible sacrifice so that we might have

Charron Monaye

freedom and life everlasting. Help us set our eyes and hearts on you, moving in a purpose of readiness and optimism. Renew our spirits; fill us with your peace and joy. We love you, and we need you this day and every day. We give you all the praise, all the glory, and all the honor, for You alone are worthy! In Jesus' Name, Amen.

Day 1: I Celebrate... Myself

"Now, I want you to stop, reflect, and just live in the moment of your victory." That is what my publicist and great friend, Madison Jaye, always tells me at the end of any event or celebration. By the time one of my events is over, you would think I would be so exhausted that I wouldn't want to do anything but sit down. Nope, not me. I would stay up planning for what's next.

Why do we ignore our wins as if they are supposed to happen? We are excited for a slight moment, but as soon as we get home and share our success on social media, it's back to business. Why don't we allow ourselves to sit and celebrate ourselves? Why don't we acknowledge our sacrifice and perseverance to ensuring the success of our projects? Is it that we take for granted the opportunity because of our egos, or is it that we are just too busy to reflect on how far we've come?

Before we can properly embark on celebrating the shifts in our lives, we must first acknowledge everything that has gone right. No matter how small you think it is or how big it may appear, I want you to celebrate it. Do you have a degree? Celebrate it. Are you able to pay your bills on time each month? Celebrate it. Do you have an employer who respects and invests in you? Celebrate it. Do you have food on your table, gas in your car, and people who love you? Celebrate it. Are both of your parents still living? Celebrate it. Has God brought you a mighty long way? Celebrate it. Were there things in your past that should have taken you out, but you are still standing healthy, strong, and wise? Celebrate it.

When we take inventory of what we have, what we have accomplished, and our ability to survive, we should celebrate it. Remember, there is always someone out there wishing they could trade places with you to have everything you take for granted. Stop wasting your energy complaining about things that probably won't matter three days from now. Instead, focus on everything you have overcome and the reward you received from it.

When Shift Happens

Today, I challenge you to reflect and take inventory. Write down everything you have overcome, everything you have, and everything you are in a position to receive. The day of allowing life to pass us by without celebrating our victories is a thing of the past. Bringing your successes to the forefront of your mind helps you focus when the shifts start to happen. They will serve as your testimony, offering you positive momentum. Nothing can stop you now!

Day 1 Journaling

I celebrate myself for never believing that I was not capable of _____

_____

_____

_____

_____

_____

_____

_____

I celebrate myself for never seeing how the loss of _____ allowed me to now have _____

_____

_____

_____

_____

_____

_____

_____

I celebrate myself for trusting the process and…

_____
_____
_____
_____
_____
_____
_____
_____
_____
_____

I celebrate myself for never giving up on myself and giving myself permission to _____

_____
_____
_____
_____
_____
_____
_____
_____
_____
_____

Day 2: I Celebrate... My Mistakes

If you are like many people, you allow your mistakes to define who you are and let them dictate just how far you can go in life. If you are like me, you allowed your mistakes to drain you, introducing you to depression and mental anxiety. Since I'm someone who does not handle stress well, my mistakes should have been the death of me. The way I used to beat myself up when I made mistakes should be a crime. From the emotional and mental beatdown that I used to put myself through, I am surprised I was able to undo all of that negative self-talk that I poured into my soul daily. I believed if I beat myself up bad enough, any judgment or ridicule anyone else offered would not stick because I had already numbed myself. However, as I started going through my transformation and learning that mistakes are merely life lessons, I began to lighten my personal attacks.

Albert Einstein once said, "Anyone who has never made a mistake has never tried anything new." This was something I had to learn and adapt to my way of thinking. Little did I know, mistakes are inevitable. Mistakes must happen. Like failures, they are the major ingredients to your success. No one walking this earth is free from making mistakes because no one is perfect. Mistakes remind us that we are human, and things are not always going to go as planned. Mistakes offer us the ability to remain the same or change to align us on the right path. If used correctly, our mistakes will generate the roadmap that will lead us straight to our goal.

Wouldn't it be amazing if life only consisted of successes and accomplishments from beginning to end? I mean, life would be easy and stress-free. Imagine life with no learning curve, regret, or disappointment. Even though that may sound great, our mistakes are the "lessons learned" needed.

As we celebrate the lessons today, I don't want you to focus on the mistakes themselves, but the success, clarity, or understanding that came from them. I am now able to set boundaries to prevent myself from repeating the same mistakes in love and relationships. Instead of being bitter, I permitted my mistakes to protect me, while giving myself enough rope to keep trying.

Today, I want you to embrace your mistakes as your playbook on what to do more of or what you should not do. Take the knowledge and grow into who you are destined to become.

Day 2 Journaling

I celebrate myself for not allowing my mistakes to…

_____

_____

_____

_____

_____

_____

_____

_____

I celebrate myself for never seeing my failure as…

_____

_____

_____

_____

_____

_____

_____

_____

I celebrate myself for trusting the process and

___

___

___

___

___

___

I celebrate myself for now being able to embrace the following mistakes:

___

___

___

___

___

___

___

___

___

___

___

___

Day 3: I Celebrate... My Heartbreak

Are you no stranger to heartbreak? Love has broken you. Life has broken you. I believe the heartbreak train hits everyone equally, if not more for others than for some. As Langston Hughes once wrote, "Life for me ain't been no crystal stair." I have been through more heartbreak than one person should ever have to experience in their lifetime. I have indeed paid my dues—from being lied to, cheated on, taken for granted, and abandoned with no explanation or proper closure. Although I have had my share of heartbreak, I was never the kind of person who allowed my experiences to deter me from loving and trusting again. However, I failed when it came to learning the lessons before starting a new relationship, thus causing me to face repeat heartbreak for the same reasons. It seemed I was living the same story but with different characters. It was like one relationship picked up where the other left off.

After a while, I grew tired of having my heart shattered. I had to sit down and figure out what the hell was wrong with me. What kind of energy, vibe, or message was I giving off that made men feel I was an easy target? Did I come off as too nice? Too naïve? Too vulnerable? Too desperate? Why was I always meeting the same type of men—those who would eventually lie, cheat, and then leave me as if I meant nothing to them. Before long, I started doubting my ability to love or be loved. Then I began questioning whether if I was asking for too much. However, when I finally took a breath and started doing some self-analyzing, I learned that my heartbreaks were a direct result of not loving myself.

Men treated me as I treated myself, like a joke. I tolerated so much in the name of love; I accepted so much in an attempt to have love. I lowered my standards just so men wouldn't find me difficult or demanding, but little did I know, they gave me what I gave myself. What was my thing with love, and why couldn't I keep it? But, when I went on my love hiatus and focused on myself, I penned the book

Love the Real You. I had to transform my need of love and learn how to be for myself what I wanted from others.

As a result, I used my heartbreaks to learn and set boundaries for myself when it came to what I would tolerate. Instead of making a list of what a man needed, I drafted a list of what I would not accept ever again. Finally finding my self-worth and love, I was no longer willing to accept less than what I could offer. After setting my new love requirements, I was now able to love myself, set the tone of what loving me looks like, and anticipate celebrating the love I knew would come.

Today, I want you to celebrate your heartbreaks by learning from them. It would be best if you didn't find fault in them but instead yourself. Remember, to celebrate life's detours and lessons, you must acknowledge and own your role in the situation. Learning what you did wrong helps you to know what to prevent later.

Day 3 Journaling

I celebrate myself for not loving myself enough to

_____

_____

_____

_____

_____

_____

_____

_____

_____

_____

_____

_____

_____

_____

I celebrate myself for never seeing how the loss of _____ was the end of my love story.

I celebrate myself for loving myself more because…

_____

_____

_____

_____

_____

_____

_____

_____

_____

I celebrate myself for using my heartbreak as a lesson to prevent me from repeating the cycle of…

_____

_____

_____

_____

_____

_____

_____

_____

_____

_____

Day 4: I Celebrate… My Divorce

Before you say, "I'm not divorced, so this chapter does not pertain to me," let me stop you. If you think I'm referring to the dissolution of a marriage, you are wrong. When it comes to this celebration journey, divorce represents your losses. Today, we are going to celebrate everything, both tangible and non-tangible, that we have lost. It is time to let go of what is no longer present in your life. Your relationship ended? Celebrate it. Your job fired you? Celebrate it. Did you lose money because of your lack of responsibly managing it? Celebrate it. We are no longer going to concern ourselves with *why* these things ended or are lost, but celebrate that they are now gone.

You are probably thinking, *Charron, are you crazy?* Yes, I may be slightly, but think about this. Only when you can accept and celebrate what is gone will you be ready to embrace the newness coming your way. You are able to position and prepare yourself for what's next. You've done the work to learn from your mistakes so that when God showers you with more blessings, you can receive them as the gifts they are. You will treasure them with a different sense of pride. You will apply what you've learned from your losses to ensure you never lose again. When you celebrate your losses, you permit yourself to live again.

A former co-worker of mine, Vaugh McNeill, once told me, "Everything in life is temporary. Everything comes with an expiration date, so enjoy the time you have with it now." I still remember my reaction. I knew death was inevitable, and we would all have to overcome losing a loved one, but going into a situation knowing it could end was something I was unwilling to accept. However, as I started meeting and connecting with people, I realized how fast things start and how they can end just as fast. Sometimes it was one-sided or mutual, but nothing was built to last, especially in business. So, with this in the back of my mind, I expected to lose. I gave myself permission to accept my losses long before they could happen. This concept made it easy for me to let go. It also allowed me to accept that everyone is not meant for me, and I am not meant for everyone. I stopped trying to force situations with people when it became clear that they would eventually leave. It was as if Vaugh was preparing me for the inevitable while challenging me to capitalize on the time given with them.

When you realize you must lose to win, you will start looking at your losses as a saving grace. When God removes those things that no longer serve you, don't try to stop Him. When God rejects something from coming to fruition, accept it. God's rejections are for your protection. So, today, celebrate what God removed from your life. I know you may miss that thing or person, but where He is about to take you, they can't come. Appreciate the peace and move forward.

Day 4 Journaling

I celebrate my divorce because it taught me…

_____

_____

_____

_____

_____

_____

_____

I celebrate my ability to now see my losses as…

_____

_____

_____

_____

_____

_____

_____

_____

I celebrate myself for trusting the process and…

_____

_____

_____

_____

_____

_____

_____

_____

_____

I celebrate myself for giving myself permission to…

_____

_____

_____

_____

_____

_____

_____

_____

_____

_____

Day 5: I Celebrate... My Childhood

How many of you had an amazing childhood? How many of you had a childhood that left you traumatized, bitter, and broken? How many of you blame your mother's choices or father's absence for the decisions you make today? When I was a paralegal, the most common excuse I heard from murderers was, "My father not being around is why I decided to kill people. I am so angry." Granted, some fathers chose to find money in the streets and take on an illegal life when they stepped up to be the man of the house and, as a result, ended up behind bars or dead, but when do we own our decisions?

I spent my teenage years in North Philadelphia,

right off 29th Street, between Cumberland and Huntington. My surroundings consisted mostly of drug dealers on the corners, dilapidated houses, poverty, and crime. However, my mother made sure we lived in a house that was considered luxurious to many. We had popcorn ceilings, cable, carpet, televisions in every room, went shopping three times a year, and ate seafood like it was cheap. Many of my friends were jealous of me and would pick on me until I let them come over or gave them something that they wanted.

Even though my childhood was great, there were still things I wish I could have changed, but I did not create a negative life for myself because of what I didn't have or couldn't do. Instead, I created what I wanted for myself. I did not blame my dad for not being around; I appreciated my mother for being there. I did not blame my mother when La'Kia and Corrine bullied me while at E. Washington Rhodes Middle School. Instead, I grew a tough shell that made it impossible for anyone's bullying to affect me. I took the many lessons or things I hated about North Philadelphia and used it as motivation to create a life that would prevent me from having to move back there. I am not a tough woman by heart, and that period in my life made me realize I needed to have a certain amount of money, a certain type of education or job, and be around a certain kind of people so I could be at peace. Now, this is no shade for those of you who enjoy the tough streets. I just know that thirteen years of living in that world taught me who I was and who I was not. It prepared me for the life I wanted and motivated me to remain on top of my game.

Look back at your childhood. What did it teach you? What have you learned about yourself based on where you have been? How did your childhood prepare and shape you into the person you are today? Did your childhood make you bitter or better? It is time to look at the lessons and address them so you can heal. Many of you are still that 5-year-old boy or girl who never got over your parents divorcing, being abandoned, being molested, being placed in foster care, being homeless, or even being broke. Many of you are holding on to all of that, not realizing that even in the midst of that pain, your purpose is the reason you are still here. There is a story you can share and a new lifestyle you can offer yourself. Don't destroy your chances of being better by carrying around eighteen years of baggage, a majority of which you could not control. Take your power back and give yourself permission to create pure joy and happiness for yourself during the next eighteen years.

Day 5 Journaling

I celebrate myself for now seeing my childhood as…

_____

_____

_____

_____

_____

_____

_____

I celebrate myself by removing all blame from my _____ and finally realizing they are no longer responsible for adult circumstances because _____

_____

_____

_____

_____

_____

_____

I celebrate myself for owning my life's…

_____

_____

_____

_____

_____

_____

_____

_____

_____

_____

I celebrate myself for forgiving myself for holding on to…

_____

_____

_____

_____

_____

_____

_____

_____

_____

Day 6: I Celebrate... My Choices

Choices! This one word was my sister's response whenever someone would complain or whine about their life or things not going right. Even though that is not what you want to hear when you are going through life's trials, it is a way for you to own your situation and do better. When we take ownership of ourselves, we permit ourselves to make the best choices. Some of us make some of the craziest, haphazard choices and wonder why things go haywire. As my mother would say, "Did you do your homework before you jumped in?" Do you budget, strategize, or thoroughly think out the situation from beginning to end? When it comes to choices, make sure you are always fully knowledgeable and equipped to handle the result of your decision. Ultimately, the choices you make will affect your future, lifestyle, freedom, and success.

However, for the purpose of celebrating, identify all of the choices you made that set you back or did not result in the wins you had planned for and prayed about. How many of you made choices based on instinct and faith, but instead of being rewarded, you felt God had failed you? Did you lose hope or analyze where you went wrong? One wrong turn can change the course of the journey. I have seen people choose to quit their job to pursue entrepreneurship, but they failed first to plan, prepare, save, and establish themselves within their given industry. But instead of owning their mistake, they blamed their friends and family for not showing support, the market for being overly saturated, and their team for not being dedicated. They blame the whole world for their loss but never take the time to ask, "What did this choice teach me? What should I have done differently so that if I decide to pursue this again, I'll be ready?"

It is time to own your choices and identify where you went wrong. Were you fully educated on what you were pursuing? Did you have money saved before you leaped? Did you discuss the opportunity with and try to gain the personal playbook of someone who already achieved what you are trying to do? How did you prepare for your choice? I don't care if you chose to start a new position, a new relationship, a new business deal, or a new lifestyle in a new state. I challenge you to celebrate the choices you made by using the data and applying it to this new opportunity to avoid making the same wrong turns. Stop looking at your unfortunate choices as setbacks. There is a saying that goes, "Your setbacks are a setup for a comeback." The celebration in your choices gives you a clear mindset and peace to learn, apply, and execute graciously. There is a level of patience and peace that covers the process, keeping you calm and steadfast during your journey. Your choices affect your life, so it's time to make better ones. Your freedom depends on it.

Day 6 Journaling

I celebrate myself for the choices I've made that negatively affected me, such as:

_____

_____

_____

_____

_____

_____

_____

_____

I celebrate myself for the choices I've made that positively affected me, such as:

_____

_____

_____

_____

_____

_____

_____

_____

I celebrate myself for not forcing things, such as:

_____
_____
_____
_____
_____
_____
_____
_____
_____

I celebrate myself for the choices I have yet to execute, believing they will…

_____
_____
_____
_____
_____
_____
_____
_____
_____
_____

Day 7: I Celebrate... My Relationships

Relationships teach us how to love, communicate, work together, and co-exist with others. They also teach us what and who we want to be in life. Relationships, whether personal, professional, or intimate, are vital to who we are. We cannot survive without having relationships where we can build, grow, and love ourselves and each other. Personally, I didn't understand the value of relationships until I became an entrepreneur and needed to build a team to assist me and have clients who purchased my services. This is where the introvert within me was challenged. Instead of embracing a network, I stayed withdrawn and kept my business to myself. Even though that took me far as a writer, it was a bit of a challenge when I decided to embark on being a playwright and book publisher. Both roles required a full team and regular clientele. To be successful in these lines of work, I had to learn how to respect the power of relationships. It was challenging at first because I had to interact with people who had different attitudes, expectations, and behaviors. Since customer service and reputations are essential to your reputation, I quickly learned that I had to set boundaries.

Even though relationships can be challenging, they teach us the most important thing that we need to learn to secure our happiness. And that is, how to love yourself. When you look back at your past relationships, you can either laugh at your choices or cry for losing them. Some of you may even be tempted to call because you miss them. Instead of focusing on how they made you feel, I challenge you to look at what they taught you about yourself. Did they teach you that you were too nice? That you were naïve and desperate? That you were not prepared for their presence and what they had to offer? What was the lesson you learned from them?

When I completed this exercise, I learned that my prior relationships treated me as I treated myself—unloving and unworthy. They did not mind hurting, manipulating, or even allowing me to take from my kids to give to them. They were okay watching me sink because I was okay with sinking. They cared for me at the level in which I cared for myself. How was this rewarding? It wasn't. When my last relationship ended, I took a long look in the mirror and asked myself one question. *Do you love yourself enough to stop being a walking billboard of self-hate?* I had to face the fact that the men I got involved with were a reflection of my self-hate for myself. I did not care about myself, so neither did they. They only told me that they loved me to keep receiving and taking what I was offering. But, in the summer of 2019, God said, "That's enough."

My outlook on relationships changed simply by me being okay with being alone. I used the downtime to learn and love me. I set boundaries and got clear on what I wanted and did not wish to have. I set rules on how to interact with me. I became a person that people either loved or hated, but the grey area of uncertainty was dead. I had wasted too much time on failed relationships, lost partnerships, and misleading connections. It was time to get clear on the people I wanted to be around and the man I wanted to love. I was not as tolerating as I was before. My shutdown-and-fallback game is ruthless. When you start choosing you, you immediately stop a lot of unnecessary foolishness.

Today, I challenge you to look at your

relationships. What are they teaching you about yourself and how you protect your happiness? Are you benefiting just as much as you are offering? If done right, relationships are beautiful connections, and it's time to celebrate the losses of what we had so that we can honor, treasure, and respect what we presently have or what is to come.

Day 7 Journaling

I celebrate myself for the relationships that I was forced to let go because _____

_____

_____

_____

_____

_____

_____

_____

_____

_____

_____

I celebrate myself for not begging, pleading, and chasing _____ to love me.

I celebrate myself for trusting the people who saw that my value would _____

_____

_____

_____

_____

_____

_____

_____

_____

_____

I celebrate myself for understanding the difference between a friend and an associate, for it saved me from _____

_____

_____

_____

_____

_____

_____

_____

Day 8: I Celebrate... My Faith

I don't know about you, but my faith has kept me sane. When shifts happened, and I was clueless about how I was going to change things around, my faith kept me motivated. It had me believe that anything was possible. It made me trust that I could handle the obstacle with grace. I was always ready to take on whatever life presented because I knew my God had my back and would not bring me this far to leave me. We may not all believe in the same God, but believing in something greater than yourself is truly life-changing. Having faith that there is a higher power who sees everything and prevents life's most challenging weapons from prospering is comforting. With life's trials and unexpected pitfalls, don't you find peace knowing that someone sits up high and watches all things?

Faith is defined in the bible as "the substance of things hoped for, the evidence of things not seen" (Hebrews 11:1). Faith is the connecting power into the spiritual realm, which links us with God and makes Him a tangible reality. For some of us, God becomes a friend, a co-pilot, or a waymaker. Our faith gives us the ability to believe that even the impossible is possible.

For years, I lived my life faithless. I knew things could happen, but my belief system was not always convinced. Thus, leading me to believe and follow the ideas, opinions, and suggestions of man. A person's validation or thought weighed more for me than mine half the time. I didn't fully believe in myself or a God to know I could do all things. I immediately broke at the sign of adversity and struggle. Although I always found a way through, it came with the price of emotional and mental pain. But then in 2015, when my dear aunt passed away, I started attending First Baptist Church of Crestmont, and Pastor Dr. Jerome F. Coleman poured the power of faith in me. His passion and testimony through his sermons made me realize that everything I was doing was because of my faith. Even though I did not always believe, I kept trying, and God never let me down. The grace of God and my faith brought me through many trials and repeated lessons I had to endure.

Attending church and Sunday School made me realize my faith was my sword of survival and achieving greatness. As long as I had faith in myself and God, there was nothing I could not do, even if I had to do it alone. I am forever indebted to my pastor, first lady, and First Baptist family for embracing a child that was walking by sight. However, when I was given permission to close my eyes and see life from what God wanted for me, that completely changed the game. I went from playing small and safe to pushing the envelope. It was the most freeing experience ever and one that led me to relocate 1,024.6 miles from home. Faith can be challenging and hard for some, but I challenge you to see for yourself what walking by faith and not by sight will do for you.

Day 8 Journaling

I celebrate myself for the ability to trust God and...

_____

_____

_____

_____

_____

_____

_____

_____

I celebrate myself for believing that God would never _____

_____

_____

_____

_____

_____

_____

_____

_____

I celebrate myself for trusting the process and…

_____
_____
_____
_____
_____
_____
_____
_____
_____
_____

I celebrate myself for walking by faith and not by sight because now I have…

_____
_____
_____
_____
_____
_____
_____
_____
_____
_____

Day 9: I Celebrate... My Vision

"Write the vision, and make it plain upon tables, that he may run who readeth it" (Habakkuk 2:2). How many of you are writing the vision? Are you making it plain so you can achieve and run with it? Many of you are sitting on the vision because you have no guarantee that it will manifest into what you desire.

Before we go forward, let's examine what having a vision means. A vision is an idea you have for yourself, your business, or anything you are manifesting. However, it's not until you get clear about your vision that it converts into the power needed to help you pursue dreams and achieve goals. Having a vision will also help you overcome obstacles when times get tough; it will keep you focused on the "why". If you do not have a vision of who you want to be or what you want out of life, you will begin to lack drive, and your life becomes just an order of events.

For me, I connect my vision to manifestation and birth it through a process. When I speak of manifesting, I'm referring to elevating the process by making it spiritual, or in other words, mentally believing that I already have it in order to attract it in the physical. I undergo this birthing process with every vision. To manifest your vision, it requires you to believe that what you want is already yours. It's like playing pretend until you obtain it. However, having the vision helps you to be grateful now for what you will manifest in the future.

Some of us expect things to happen, and when it does, it's no big deal. God answered your prayers, and without thinking any more about it, you move on to the next thing that you desire. But, when you are manifesting, you are mentally and emotionally preparing for it. Even though you expect it, the gratitude in receiving it is heightened because you know what you are asking for is going to change your worth in life.

I do not play small; everything I envision for myself is impossible for me. I might lack something that keeps me from making it a reality today, but the way I manifest, I make a liar out of myself every time, eventually achieving whatever I set out to do. I have become so good at manifesting that I had to hire a whole business team because life is just that amazing. Are you living your vision, or are you still watching your dreams pass by?

Right now, I want you to celebrate how your visions have manifested in your life, but I want to offer you the opportunity to elevate the idea. If you envisioned being debt-free, I want you now to envision financial freedom and having an abundance of wealth. Getting out of debt is not enough; you should want more.

We should live our lives as if we have everything we need while preparing for what we want. That way, when we finally receive what we've been working towards, we can enjoy it.

What are you manifesting that you could be grateful for now? It is time to create the receiving energy that attracts you to the lifestyle, freedom, love, and abundance you have been praying to receive. Like James 2:26 says, "Faith without works is dead." You can believe you already have what you want, but you still have to work to get it. So, as we celebrate the vision, let's remember to dream big, live as if you have already achieved the impossible, and enjoy the fruits of your labor. You deserve it.

Day 9 Journaling

I celebrate myself for my thought and beliefs about…

_____

_____

_____

_____

_____

_____

_____

I celebrate myself for trusting the plans God has for me, such as…

_____

_____

_____

_____

_____

_____

_____

I celebrate myself for believing that I am worthy to…

___

___

___

___

___

___

___

___

___

I am so happy and grateful to be receiving…

___

___

___

___

___

___

___

___

___

Day 10: I Celebrate... My Finances

If you have an emergency fund, a credit card with a zero balance, a retirement fund, and a credit score of 800 or higher, stand up and celebrate your hard work. If you don't, I still want you to celebrate in advance for your financial breakthrough that is yet to come. For many, finances are the number one reason why they can't progress in life. They possess the desire, the drive, and the opportunity to have the lifestyle they want, but they can't afford it. Don't you hate it? You are so close, yet so far.

In the opening chapter, I shared that I have had troubling finances off and on for years. From destroying my credit in college, having my credit further damaged during my marriage, having a judgment against me, falling into the trap of payday loans, and maxing out credit cards—I have experienced it all. My expenses always outweighed my income, so legally getting more money was vital. Hell, one of the reasons I have so many degrees was for the refund checks. I just never had enough money.

However, in 2014, when my poor financial decisions nearly caused my children and me to be homeless, it was time for me to rewrite the narrative on my finances. I became married to finances, almost to the point of obsession. I studied, took courses, read books, and watched webinars on pursuing financial freedom. I learned from Suzie Orman, Dave Ramsey, and Nicole Lapin. From budget planning to using the snowball method, I went from having a credit score of 500 with collections, judgments, and derogatory accounts on my report to making it to the 700 Club with 100% on-time payments and all negative accounts removed.

Now, it wasn't easy. I hustled my services and sacrificed spending time with my kids to work so I could clean up what was hindering us. I could not afford the life I was living with the circumstances I was in, so I had to change it.

When the shift happens, your finances are the

number one thing that will save you. Your funds are your lifeline to being able to enjoy life the way you desire. Wouldn't it be amazing to take a cruise on the Atlantic Ocean on your yacht while enjoying wine and grapes? Wouldn't it be wonderful if you could afford the house and car you wanted, paid in full at the time of purchase? How would you feel if you had no debt and could maintain 100% of your net salary? How you celebrate your money will dictate just how much living you will be able to do.

Since I got ahead of my finances and started living below my means, it has afforded me the ability to live freely. I can travel when I want, buy what I want, and enjoy life how I want. When you give yourself permission to enjoy money, without owing anyone, that is when you will know you have arrived. Even though I still have student loans and a car note, I have available finances that allow me to celebrate the life I warranted.

Today, I want you to put a plan in place to get your financial situation in order. Do the work and sacrifice if you have to, but don't stop until you are at a place that can offer you the freedom to enjoy the money you earn. It is time to break the financial bondage chains so you can complete your bucket list and live happily ever after.

Day 10 Journaling

I celebrate myself for manifesting extra commas on my available balance by _____

_____

_____

_____

_____

_____

_____

I celebrate myself for understanding how I view money so I can now _____

_____

_____

_____

_____

_____

_____

_____

I celebrate myself for believing that I am worthy of wealth because _____

_____

_____

_____

_____

_____

_____

_____

_____

_____

I celebrate myself for seeing my finances as freedom so I can _____

_____

_____

_____

_____

_____

_____

_____

_____

Day 11: I Celebrate... My Intention

What does it mean to be intentional? Being intentional is attaching purpose to your life. Everything you say and do has some form of meaning or fulfillment for you. You are not living for the sole purpose of being liked and loved; you have created a strategic plan that guides you to peace. Just like when you have a vision, intentional living requires you to get clear on what you want. You can't be intentional yet unaware of why you are doing what you are doing. You can't be ready to buy a house but unsure as to why you would benefit from it. Being intentional challenges you to appreciate life for what it is, a gift worth enjoying.

Each New Year's Eve, Dr. Jerome F. Coleman, the pastor of First Baptist Church of Crestmont, gives us a slogan for the next year to help us get and stay in alignment with God's purpose for our lives. I believe it was New Year's Eve 2018, and Pastor Coleman set the tone for 2019 with the slogan, "Be Intentional." When I heard that, I went straight into understanding what that meant and how I needed to apply it to my life. As I started researching and learning, I found that to be intentional was nothing more than making every decision matter. The day of "just existing" was over. The day of doing things "just because I can" was over. For everything I did, I would ask myself, "Why are you doing this?" There had to be a reason attached to everything. This was new to me. I used to be the type of person who did what I wanted because I could, and nobody could stop me. If I wanted it, I got it. I did not focus on the consequences or consider the repercussions. I lived in haste, not with purpose. However, as I grew into the habit of asking myself why, my life developed purpose that gravitated people to me. It was like those who only saw me before made it their business to speak to me now. Being intentional not only made me attractive, but it also elevated my business.

Just like anything else, being intentional requires work. You can no longer move when you want, but only when it's necessary. You think more about what you are about to agree to before saying yes. You are more cautious and appreciative of life while enjoying the purpose behind it. Being intentional also gives you permission not to be perfect and to be okay with it. Intentional living is allowing yourself to grow in purpose while learning what is best for you. It's removing the pressure of society's expectations and generational traditions and applying your tranquility to who you are becoming. Since having become purposeful, I have released tons of stress, my edges are flourishing, and my anxiety is low. It either works, or it doesn't. But it's not my goal to force it. Purpose is not forced; it is celebrated.

So, today, I want to challenge you to be intentional. Give your life purpose and watch how things evolve. Motivate yourself to believe that what you seek is yours. You are connected to a greater purpose in life, and it is your job to find what your greater purpose is. Why were you born? What gift did God impregnate you with that is now time to birth? When you can answer these questions, only then will you be able to become clear on your intent and transform your life into what will benefit you during and after your pursuit.

Day 11 Journaling

I celebrate myself being intentional by the way I…

_____

_____

_____

_____

_____

_____

_____

_____

I celebrate myself for understanding that moving with intent will _____

_____

_____

_____

_____

_____

_____

_____

I celebrate myself for removing everything that goes against _____

_____
_____
_____
_____
_____
_____
_____
_____

I celebrate myself for seeing how my intentions, if selfish motives are involved, can _____

_____
_____
_____
_____
_____
_____
_____
_____
_____

Day 12: I Celebrate... My Love

Let me start by saying I am no expert at love, nor do I have the perfect love story to share. However, I have experienced enough to know that love is something I am passionate about and will fight for.

My love story started back when I was fifteen years old. His name was Charles Gardner; my aunt Tracey called him Chuck. He was two years older than me, but Chuck was the most handsome, funniest, and caring guy ever. My parents liked him, so I was allowed to go places with him. He would also come over the house, and I would go over to his. His mother was the sweetest woman. You couldn't tell me that I had not met my soulmate. That is until I received the call that set the tone of how love worked.

It was about a year and a half into our relationship, and I was starting my college search journey. Chuck called, saying he had to talk. *Ut-oh!* He shared with me that he had enlisted in the Air Force so he could provide for his son that was on the way. I quickly became confused because I was not pregnant. *So who is she?* I thought. Apparently, he had started seeing his old girlfriend again, and one night of pleasure resulted in a life-changing decision. I cried uncontrollably, and he apologized profusely until I hung up the phone. My first encounter with love created my perception that all men were cheaters, and since I put that in the universe for myself, it became my reality with almost every person I dated or every relationship I got into after that.

From the cheating to the lying, it was like I had manifested the golden ticket for how men were supposed to treat me. It was as if once they gained access to me, permission was granted for them to cheat on me, lie to me, and manipulate me into believing we would share a life that was never going to manifest. It wasn't until 2015, when I learned that a guy who I was dating had gotten married on me, that I took a step back to figure out why I kept getting the same result every time I tried my hand at love. It was like I was preparing these men to be other women's husbands.

Was I too helpful? Was I not supposed to hold my man down? Was I coming across as being too needy? I never cheated or stepped wrong in a relationship, so why was I the target?

It took me writing my book, *Love the Real You*, to finally understand that even though I was not a cheater, I was cheating myself out of love. I was staying too long, accepting too much, and tolerating things that weren't for me. I was raising men and financially supporting them, thinking they would see me as a "real one". Instead, I was cleaning them up for the women they really wanted. After that revelation, my tolerance got shorter, and my desire to sacrifice my happiness just to have someone changed. No more being there for someone who was barely there for me. Granted, I am still the loving and giving woman I was because that is who I am. But I am no longer going to stay in a relationship alone. I will never beg for what you say you want but are too busy to reciprocate. You can't take from me and not fill me back up with your love, affection, and security. I will not be the only one in a relationship who has the other's back. I have learned that I am not for everyone. I want what I want, and there is no longer room for compromise.

Today, I celebrate Chuck for setting the tone of

love for me. I have accepted a lot, been through so much, and ignored much more, but now I celebrate my ability to know the love I want. I know what it looks like—from how it feels to how it admires me when I come home. I have experienced enough wrong to know what is right and what I deserve. I celebrate every bad relationship as great moments because I am now clear in my heart about what love is for me.

Today, I want you to look back over your love life and get clear on what love looks like for you. If you are married, congratulations! Still, get clear so you can be sure you are receiving in return what you are giving in your marriage. It's okay to compromise for a relationship but never for your heart.

Day 12 Journaling

I celebrate myself for the ability to love in spite of…

_____

_____

_____

_____

_____

_____

_____

_____

I celebrate myself for trusting that my soulmate is...

_____

_____

_____

_____

_____

_____

_____

_____

_____

I celebrate myself for knowing that I am worthy of love because _____

_____
_____
_____
_____
_____
_____
_____
_____
_____
_____
_____
_____
_____
_____
_____

I celebrate myself for never giving up on myself even after _____ left me.

Day 13: I Celebrate... My Enemies

"Keep your friends close and your enemies closer" is a saying I heard often while growing up and still do to this day. When I became an adult, this saying became more relevant because I needed to stay five steps ahead of folks. People tend to be slick, malicious, and unpredictable, and since their actions can affect my life, knowing their next move is necessary.

This day may make some of you look at me strangely because I am asking you to celebrate and embrace your enemies, or haters as they refer to them today. However, when you know who your enemies are and understand why your haters are hating, you can change the game using their motivation and desire to see you fail. Even God gave you the comfort of knowing that your enemies are supposed to elevate you when He said in Psalm 110:1, "The LORD says to my Lord: "Sit at my right hand until I make your enemies a footstool for your feet."

We all need enemies and haters in our lives. I used to tell my children, "Your enemies confirm your success by the amount of hate they have for you." I don't know about you, but I require enemies and haters in my life. I learn a lot about myself and my business. I know when I am winning and when I am not. I know when I am closer to my goal and when I need to do more work. Depending on the amount of interest they show in what I'm doing, it helps me gauge if I'm far from my goal and need to do some adjusting or if I am right on the money. I love my haters and enemies because, in addition to my manifesting and hard work, their continued support, or lack thereof, has helped get me to where I am today.

Let's not forget the ones who try to discourage you by telling you that you will never be successful or that the goal you have set is out of your reach. If you have heard any of my interviews, I make it clear that people telling me what I cannot do is the fuel I need to explode and leave all their mouths hanging open. I love it when people doubt me. When they do, I make it my life's purpose to prove them wrong, and I do it in a way that is purposeful for me.

Your enemies serve no purpose in life other than to give you the motivation to keep going forward. Some of you allow your enemies to deter, deny, and destroy your dreams and visions for yourself. They sell you a reality based on their projection of themselves. I have come to believe that enemies don't like you because you had the courage to achieve their dreams. You made what they desire look easy to achieve, and since you are not putting them on, you are worth their hate. Many people want what you have and are mad that you have it and not them. Misery loves company, so they try to hold you back from reaching your goals.

I enjoy haters and welcome them daily. I need some new motivation! As we celebrate our haters, let us remember their purpose. They are nothing more than elevators for us to use to reach the top. Step up and move on.

Day 13 Journaling

I celebrate myself for keeping my enemies close because _____

_____

_____

_____

_____

_____

_____

_____

_____

I celebrate myself for not allowing my enemies to…

_____

_____

_____

_____

_____

_____

_____

I celebrate myself for believing that God sent my enemies so I could _____

_____
_____
_____
_____
_____
_____
_____
_____

I celebrate myself for have the courage to celebrate my enemies in spite of _____

_____
_____
_____
_____
_____
_____
_____
_____

Day 14: I Celebrate… My Job, Career, or Work

This chapter will not focus on encouraging you to stay at your place of employment, but instead how to use your job to elevate your personal life goals. I am not from the old school where they tell you to go to school, graduate, get a job, retire at age 65, and enjoy life the best you can while living on a fixed income. I don't know about you, but that's not for me!

I look at employment as the investor of your dream. When I started Pen Legacy, I was unemployed. I had no capital, no clients, and no business plan. All I had was a vision and my pen to publish books, write scripts, and compose songs. I could not afford a coach, and I did not have fancy marketing material; I had an idea. When I became employed, though, I used my paycheck to build my business. Google was my coach, and my job was my client that paid me faithfully every other week. My money was even direct deposited. How could I go wrong with this?

Even though everyone is not cut out to be an entrepreneur, this world continues to show us that we cannot depend on our job or government assistance. Our ability to provide is up to us. We are being challenged more and more to become our own bosses and pursue our dreams. Having multiple streams of income is no longer a conversation for entrepreneurs; it's about survival.

During the 2018 recession, an estimated 2.6 million jobs were lost, and about 10 million Americans lost their homes. Right now, we are facing a pandemic where the coronavirus has eliminated 36.5 million jobs in two months. In both years, no one foresaw something like this happening, and most were not financially prepared. Why? Because we are taught to depend on our jobs. We're told not to pursue our gift because it's not a guaranteed and consistent source of income. Work! Work! Work! With losing their jobs, how will these people survive? Our parents taught us how to live, but who can teach us how to survive in a world that is losing rapidly to viruses, technology, and outsourcing?

Today, I want you to celebrate your job, career, or work as a platform to help you create another income source. What transferrable skills can you use to embark on creating something you will enjoy doing while making money? Can you cook, write, sing? Can you tutor children? What can you do to start depending on yourself rather than standing in an unemployment line or at a food bank seeking assistance? How long are you going to live your life at the mercy of someone else?

If you don't want to start a business, you can always invest in someone else's and make money as they grow. Our government should not have to remind you that you are thirty seconds away from unemployment. Your family depends on you to provide for them today, not when the government can process your application. Let's shift our thinking regarding our jobs and see them as the passport now to more money tomorrow. Let your paycheck be the down payment to your future. Invest it now!

Day 14 Journaling

I celebrate myself for seeing my employer as an investor to _____

_____

_____

_____

_____

_____

_____

_____

I celebrate myself for being able to leverage my job so I can now _____

_____

_____

_____

_____

_____

_____

_____

I celebrate myself for using my ability to network to
_____
_____
_____
_____
_____
_____
_____
_____
_____

I celebrate myself for positioning myself for my dream career where I am _____
_____
_____
_____
_____
_____
_____
_____
_____
_____
_____

Day 15: I Celebrate... My Marriage

Let me start by saying I enjoyed being married. It's a great feeling to know that you have a helpmate with whom you can experience, enjoy, and grow through life together. Marriage is a union that allows you to travel through life with someone who has your back during all of its detours and lessons. Even though I am patiently waiting for God to send my forever husband, I celebrate every day as if he is already here. I am a sucka for love and look forward to the day when I wake up every day next to someone who makes me feel like I don't have to do this alone. Being a strong and independent woman, I get tired of living life solo. I always have to make the choices, execute the choices, and prepare for the consequences of the choices, whether good or bad. It's exhausting, but I am patient because my next marriage will be 'til death do us part.

Since I am not married, I will not drag out this section, but I do want you to take some time out to appreciate your spouse. I challenge you to write down everything they do that has made your life rewarding and easier to handle. Acknowledge how they have inspired and encouraged you to grow outside of your comfort zone.

Today, spontaneously create a date night and share your gratitude while enjoying each other's company. Despite everything that is going on around us, you are blessed to have someone who loves you, provides for you, and cares for you. Your spouse sees your good and bad, and they accept you with all your flaws. It's not because they have to; it's because they love you and respect their vows. Far too often, we forget to take a minute from the rat race to say thank you. So, take that moment today.

Remember to use every day as an opportunity to celebrate your marriage and your spouse. It will definitely keep a happier home!

Day 15 Journaling

I celebrate myself for being open to sharing my life with _____

_____

_____

_____

_____

_____

_____

I celebrate myself for allowing myself the ability to be vulnerable to _____

_____

_____

_____

_____

_____

_____

_____

I celebrate myself for trusting the process and…

_____

_____

_____

_____

_____

_____

_____

_____

_____

I celebrate myself for forgiving my spouse and saying no to _____

_____

_____

_____

_____

_____

_____

_____

_____

_____

Day 16: I Celebrate... My Failures

Failure isn't fatal. It is REQUIRED for progression and success. Failing is where you get some of your best lessons and develop your playbook of life. However, failing forward is where you gain the best outcome and the greatest reward. It's because it strengthens certain attributes that you fail to use.

What is failing forward? Failing forward is nothing more than understanding how to leverage your mistakes, evaluating what went wrong, and adjusting to what should have been done. It makes you analyze, strategize, and get persistent when it comes to achieving your goal. When you understand the lesson behind the loss, you gain much valuable information that will help you win and help you rise to a level you once thought was out of your reach.

Just like with your mistakes, when celebrating your failures, you permit yourself to be imperfect and human—the two things we beat ourselves up for being. I am not sure who told you that being human was a crime, and why we cringe at being anything other than perfect. I often tell people my imperfections make me the ideal human to live life. I have accepted who I am. I don't have the time or energy to pretend to be someone I am not, only for someone else to find fault and dislike me anyway. It's natural for me to be myself, whether you like, love, or hate it. Celebrating your failures is honoring who you are as a person. Not saying there is no room for improvement because there is, but only improve on the things that make you unique, such as your character, values, and behavior. It is time for you to be okay with being okay.

I don't always get it right in business, love, on the job, or being a mother. But, I can't allow my failures to stop me. Even though failing hurts, it gives me the tools to make smarter choices, eliminate what doesn't work, and implement what I have learned. I now embrace failing. Call me crazy, but I do.

Failing has afforded me the opportunity to learn to coach and become a coach to many who are ready

When Shift Happens

to achieve what I have while bypassing the trials that I endured. I often tell people that I tried and tested life so that you don't have to. As an author and entrepreneur, I have spent close to a million dollars due to my lack of knowledge, resources, and desire to keep trying. From paying for coaches but failing, then paying to try it again and still failing, I would not want that for my evilest enemy. It's one thing to want a legacy, but it's another thing to lose almost everything while pursuing it. Now, I am unstoppable when it comes to being an author and entrepreneur. I have mastered the industry and the business of customer service, marketing, business law, branding, and maintaining a company. My business has been open since December 5, 2008, and today, we have gained numerous clients, multiple awards, and plenty of profits. This is what failing while learning will do. However, since it is not my goal to have everyone lose the way I did, I coach people the right way so they can skip the failing and float straight to the bank.

Are you ready to learn and collect real-time data on what you are missing or how to make it better? If so, why are you so afraid of failing? If you want to be successful, you must fail, and you must fail forward. The forward keeps you pushing; it is what keeps you in the race and moving closer to your goal. No one has ever become successful without failing, so why do you think you will be able to do it without error? Embrace the failure and find comfort in knowing that in the end, your reward will be one you never imagined.

Day 16 Journaling

I celebrate myself for not allowing my failures to…

_____

_____

_____

_____

_____

_____

_____

_____

I celebrate myself for not letting my failures to define me, but instead to _____

_____

_____

_____

_____

_____

_____

_____

_____

I celebrate myself for seeing my failures as…

_____
_____
_____
_____
_____
_____
_____
_____
_____
_____

I celebrate myself for embracing my failures by…

_____
_____
_____
_____
_____
_____
_____
_____
_____

Day 17: I Celebrate... My Life

Life is the most precious gift anyone could ever be given, even with all of its unpredictable twists and turns. I don't know about you, but with everything I have been through, celebrated, overcame, and built, my life is still important. Some of us take life for granted, not thinking it can be cut short today, tomorrow, or in the next second. We live like tomorrow is promised.

A majority of us don't truly enjoy life to its fullest potential because we find ways to discourage our pursuit of it. We have fifty states within the United States, and you would be surprised how many people have never traveled outside of their state. There are seven continents on the globe, but how many people do you know traveled to another continent? Better yet, how many have a passport? Why don't we enjoy life? Is it because we are raised to go to school, work, have a family, retire, and wait to die? Why don't we live outside of our comfort zone and explore the world?

My oldest son is currently stationed in Hawaii, his first duty station outside of living in Philadelphia and briefly in Florida. He completed boot camp in South Carolina and advanced individual training in Georgia. As a kid, he traveled with me to New York, New Jersey, Delaware, Maryland, DC, and Los Angeles. My children were raised exploring life and seeing what the world has to offer. Chris's favorite saying is from one of Drake's songs: *"I am here for a good time, not for a long time."* When I first heard him say that, I flipped because I took it as death was approaching. But, when I understood it from his perspective, I agreed. Death has no estimated time of arrival, so it's best to live life to the fullest.

Life is all about learning, living, celebrating, and planting enough seeds to leave a legacy before our time is up. Most of the other stuff we focus on is so irrelevant. If it doesn't add to your life and legacy, why give it such importance? I would rather enjoy life and plant a legacy for my children than stress over the everyday trials of life that I know will happen whether I worry about them or not.

When Shift Happens

Some of you live life stressed out over bills, heartbreak, others driving too slow, your boss getting on your nerves, your neighbors being trifling, or my favorite one, regrets. Can I share a secret? All of that can be changed. You can pay your bills, make better relationship choices, understand that everything is not a race, find a new job, move to a new neighborhood, and invest in your dreams. The things you complain about are things you can change. I hate complaining with a passion! If you don't intend to change, then please shut up about whatever you are complaining about. I even catch myself when I am about to complain and instead say, "I'm grateful." I use the phrase "I'm grateful" as a placeholder to keep me still while I work on making changes. With everything God has blessed me with, I do not have the right to complain about anything. However, if I am tired of the situation, I know how to excuse myself.

So, today, LIVE! Stop complaining. Stop focusing on everything wrong. It's time to embrace Drake's line: *"I am here for a good time, not for a long time."* And a good time is what I intend to have.

Day 17 Journaling

I celebrate myself for accepting who I am in spite of…

_____

_____

_____

_____

_____

_____

_____

I celebrate myself for being able to achieve…

_____

_____

_____

_____

_____

_____

_____

_____

I celebrate myself for trusting God did not bring me this far to…

_____
_____
_____
_____
_____
_____
_____
_____
_____

I celebrate myself for life's obstacles because they have taught me that…

_____
_____
_____
_____
_____
_____
_____
_____
_____

Day 18: I Celebrate... My Ability to Relocate

"If you want to be successful in your business, you will have to leave Philadelphia. People don't support their own until they become successful somewhere else first."

I can remember hearing this often while building my business, Pen Legacy. From the music to the books to the plays to becoming a book publisher, I always wondered why Atlanta supported me more than Philly. Why did New York embrace me, and Philly didn't? What I had been told started to ring true, and that was the start of my desire to leave. I didn't relocate because I wanted to, but I knew I had to if I ever wanted to be successful.

Charron Monaye

When it comes to relocating, some people are forced to move because of their job or want a fresh start. In my case, it was to enhance my business and explore the world outside of the 215. I love my city, but after I started traveling with my business, I realized there is so much life outside of South Street. Since I am a mother and employee, I had to get strategic on how I would make the move happen for us.

I was not financially prepared to pick up and move, solely depending on the income from Pen Legacy. With that reality, I decided to use my employer as leverage to get me where I needed to be. With my employer having offices in every state, I just had to decide which state I wanted to move to and when. With my mommy hat on, I decided the best time would be after my oldest son graduated from high school. So, I started planning and preparing.

When I rekindled a prior relationship back in 2015, my desire to relocate almost became a reality because he was in the Army and stationed in Texas. With me traveling back and forth to see him, I started learning that area, and of course, my job had an office in Houston. Perfect!

With the hope of us being together, I started cleaning out and packing up my house. I even sold some stuff. I had my job; Houston would be great for my business, and I was in love. Again, perfect. HA!

When that relationship started fading, I kept my same energy, reminding myself that I had promised when Chris graduated, we were out. Plus, I had thrown away so much that we were already two feet out of Philadelphia. So, I started applying for out-of-state promotions within my company and got hired for the authorizer position at the St. Petersburg regional office. Then I was offered the same job in Seattle, but the timing was not right.

But then, I received the rater job at the St. Petersburg regional office, and I requested a delay in relocation so my kids could finish out the school year and graduate. Jackpot!

With no family in Wesley Chapel, Florida, I took the leap of faith on July 16, 2019. Even though I was excited to have manifested, prepared, and planned for this day, the reality hit that it was the first time in my life that I would be this far from my parents and family. I was moving to a state alone. No support. No friends. Just me trusting a dream.

Picking up and leaving the life you know behind to start a new one can be intimidating and scary, but when you have done the work to prepare and plan, the impossible becomes possible. If relocating is in your cards, my biggest advice would be to start early. Make sure you have a moving fund, emergency fund, and enough belief in yourself to know you can do it.

If you have already taken the leap to relocate, I celebrate with you on the new life, and I know you have a lot to celebrate. Life gives us the ability to move and make choices that are beneficial for us. Florida was never on my radar to make home, but God saw otherwise. Leap! I am here to tell you this has been one of the best decisions I have made for myself in an exceptionally long time. I am still not sure if this is my forever home, but it's home for now.

Day 18 Journaling

I celebrate myself for stepping out on faith to…

_____

_____

_____

_____

_____

_____

_____

_____

I celebrate myself for trusting that God has a plan for me to…

_____

_____

_____

_____

_____

_____

_____

_____

I celebrate myself for my ability to dream past my…

_____

_____

_____

_____

_____

_____

_____

_____

_____

I celebrate myself for being able to live outside of my comfort zone by…

_____

_____

_____

_____

_____

_____

_____

_____

_____

Day 19: I Celebrate...
Change

"The great courageous act that we must all do, is to have the courage to step out of our history and past so that we can live our dreams."

~ Oprah Winfrey

Maybe you can help me with this question. Why are we so afraid of change? Is it because we don't like the feeling of being unprepared for the unknown? Or is it that we don't believe we deserve what's coming?

When I speak about shifts happening, I am referring to nothing more than change. Change is inevitable. Just like the seasons of the year, change is a part of our lives. It keeps us unique and gives us the ability to learn daily. Have you ever driven the same route home, but one particular day a road was closed, forcing you to take a detour? At first, you may have yelled and cursed because you thought the detour was taking you out of the way. But low and behold, you got to your destination sooner. When you give yourself permission to accept a detour in life, you open yourself to the possibility of reaching your destination faster. You may also eliminate some pitfalls or setbacks by agreeing to change your route in life.

Now I know you may be thinking, *But it's comfortable here.* It may be, but do you desire a life of comfort or one that is extraordinary? Why settle for less when there is a whole world out there waiting to greet you? When you embrace change, you begin the journey of freedom and having a lifestyle that comes with success and happiness. It's as if God starts rewarding you for finally trusting Him.

Since moving to Florida, I have been able to get so much accomplished. My lifestyle has grown, my business has flourished, and my trust in my abilities has heightened. I no longer play myself short because I have the receipts of what change can do. Now don't get me wrong, there will be hills and valleys that you may have to go through as change takes place, but those obstacles will keep you motivated to move forward. For me, the hills and valleys are the most important part of change because they hold the key to the lessons needed to keep you afloat. They are the ingredients to the playbook that you will use as your testimony or a reminder for what not to do.

Change forces you to pay attention to what went wrong and holds you accountable for fixing it. Change can be your worst enemy or your closet friend, but no matter how you view it, you need to get familiar with who you need change to be in your life.

As we celebrate change, I want to offer you the Serenity Prayer by Reinhold Niebuhr. Allow it to serve as comfort and reassurance as you go through change.

God grant me the serenity to accept the things I cannot change;
courage to change the things I can; and
wisdom to know the difference.

I understand change can be scary, but as long as you trust God, believe in yourself, and know what you can and cannot do, I promise you what's about to come will be better than what you left.

Day 19 Journaling

I celebrate myself for my ability to change, because it has afforded me the opportunity to…

_____

_____

_____

_____

_____

_____

_____

I celebrate myself for seeing change as inevitable, freeing me from…

_____

_____

_____

_____

_____

_____

_____

I celebrate myself for welcoming change so that I can continue to receive…

_____

_____

_____

_____

_____

_____

_____

_____

_____

I celebrate myself for never giving up on myself and giving myself permission to…

_____

_____

_____

_____

_____

_____

_____

_____

_____

_____

Day 20:
I Forgive Myself Letter

"The greatest gift of surrender was that it helped me to realize that it is arrogant of me not to forgive myself when God forgives me."

~ *Iyanla Vanzant*

For the past 21 days, I have challenged you to see the celebration in every unexpected shift that life has placed upon you. Some days may have been harder than others, but I hope you found strength and courage in letting go of the pain. Don't you think it's time to refill your mind, body, and spirit with positivity and readiness? Remember, what you believe to be true will remain your reality even if it's a false reality. To celebrate in life, we must see life for what it is and be okay with knowing that even though things will happen to us, it will also work out for your good.

For Day 20, write a heartfelt letter giving yourself permission to forgive yourself for all that you have allowed, tolerated, accepted, and offered individuals. I want you to go deep to the haunting memories that are subconsciously preventing you from living the life you desire. Use this day to allow your heart to break. Give that little girl permission to weep so the adult can protect her. Offer the adult the voice to release what has been holding you hostage for years. As you let your pen cry on the lines that follow the end of this section, know that I also had to complete this exercise, and more than once, to get to a place of fully owning my life. We can't move in freedom if we are holding on to things that are beyond our control. It happened; it sucked; it's over. You learned so you can grow. Your tomorrow is waiting for you to show up at your highest potential. You can do this!

So, grab your tissue box, a cup of tea, and prepare yourself for the biggest breakthrough. Release everything you are holding on to—from regret, guilt, shame, pain, and heartbreak. You are bigger than your past. So, it's time to rise above. Forgiveness is for your freedom, not theirs, and where life is trying to take you will require you to be baggage-free. Break free so you can live freely!

Day 21: Permission Slip of Life

In the book *Abundance Now*, motivational speaker and best-selling author Lisa Nichols wrote, "I have nothing to hide! I have nothing to protect! I have nothing to prove! I have nothing to defend! Now…who do I choose to be?" I used her words as my tool to become the woman you see today.

Who do I choose to be? That question alone made me reconsider the answer to my "why". Understanding the relevance behind this work gave me the permission needed to accept who I would become after the work was complete. Your "why" is vital to how you respond and consistently work on yourself even after the 21 days are over. Self-growth is not a one and done; it is a lifestyle. We are trying to break generational curses, self-sabotaging thoughts, disappointment, the pain inflicted by others, and projected fears that have suffocated our growth. When you think about it, we are a big pile of mess. And we wonder why our lives are in turmoil. Look at everything you are carrying.

Today, though, we are going to give ourselves permission to live, especially since we did the work yesterday to forgive ourselves.

Today, I want you to reward yourself by sharing your goals, visions, hopes, dreams, love, and prayers for the person you are now choosing to become. You deserve to know what's ahead of you so you can plan accordingly to receive it, while at the same time being ready for any shifts life may bring. It is time to have what you always prayed for and what God ordained for you, and have the ability just to be grateful. See the good in what was intended for evil.

Today, offer yourself the courage and permission to love yourself to no end. After you celebrate by manifesting your goal list using the space at the end of this chapter, go and have a great day on purpose. Get your hair and nails done; get a manicure and pedicure; get a massage; sign up for a gym membership; have a solo lunch date at the most expensive restaurant without worrying about the menu prices. Today, it's about celebrating and preparing for your life to come.

Allow today to be the start of your freedom. Get intentional about your next steps and prepare mentally, emotionally, and physically for the journey, because I am here to warn you, the devil will get busy. Your happiness will insult him, causing him to attempt to trick you, distract you with delays, and throw obstacles your way. But, if you prepare as you execute, his weapons will never gain traction. They will just become steps that will elevate you and help get you to your destiny faster!

GOALS:

_____

_____

_____

_____

_____

_____

_____

_____

_____

Charron Monaye

Thank you for taking this journey with me! Wishing you Peace & Blessings to your new life.

Charron Monaye

Acknowledgements

With love and gratitude, I would like to thank and acknowledge my supportive children, Christopher and Craig. No matter how I showed up as a mother, you've never judged me or made me feel like I was inadequate. You embraced my decisions and trusted me enough to remain by my side no matter what. Thank you for your unconditional love and support as I embarked on my life as an entrepreneur and author. You believed in my gifts enough to witness your mother live out a dream of seeing her stage play premiere in Hollywood, California. Your unwavering support and forgiveness demand so much honor and gratitude. Let's celebrate the sacrifice and enjoy our new life in paradise. Love you.

To my parents, even though my mother encouraged me to write and my dad dared me to be great, this journey has been rewarding. Did you ever think the little girl who performed her poem at the NAACP banquet would have her books published in the Library of Congress? This pen has brought me a long way, from news outlets, music to theater, and books. I pray my legacy has made you proud.

To my sister, Cheryl, even though we have had our ups and downs, we are still collectively leaving our mark in the world. I am super proud of your success and how you are growing into the woman that God intended you to be. Thank you for your support and for being an "extra" in my play. We may be unique in our own way, but we are still cut from the same cloth. Success awaits.

To my love, Martin, thank you for offering me a different perspective on life. Thank you for loving me despite my flaws and teaching me how to focus on what matters. No one is perfect, and life will happen. But if we put our trust in God, believe in His Word, and honor His plan, there is nothing we cannot achieve. I may be rough around the edges, but know that the interior is pure and open to what's next. Cheers to growing in love.

To my aunts, uncles, cousins, and granny, thank you for your support. Sending a special thanks to my aunts, Arlean Sadler and Margaret Tolliver. Even though you are no longer here with us, your teachings, lessons, and presence remain. I appreciate the continued guidance you offer daily.

To my Pen Legacy Team and Family, you all rock. I know I am not the easiest to work with, but for some reason, you all remain! Love you!

To my coaches, Tiana Von Johnson, Toni Moore, Esq., Lucinda Cross-Otiti, Brittany Garth, and Dr. Syleecia Thompson. You all have encouraged, influenced, and shared a part in my transformation. This place of clarity and celebration took work, and even though I am not where I want to be fully, I am not far away. Thank you!

To my pastor, Dr. Jerome F. Coleman, the man who changed my whole perspective on God and my life. Although First Baptist Church of Crestmont was a family church for me, it did not click that it was home until 2015 during my unexpected season. I appreciate you and First Lady Kim Coleman for your delivery of God's word so that I could apply it and now celebrate within it. Thank you!

To everyone who has ever supported me by purchasing a book, seeing one of my plays, or hiring me to publish, ghostwrite, or coach you, thank you. With the vast options of reaching your goals of success, I am grateful you chose me. I hope that I served you well!

About The Author

From humble beginnings to being a highly sought-after writer, Charron Monaye continues to exemplify excellence while expanding her interests in marketing, coaching, film, and beyond. This bestselling author and groundbreaking writing expert has evolved into a Who's Who in America's Arts and Literature.

As a dynamic businesswoman and writer with over twenty-seven years in the industry, Charron and her pen are a force to be reckoned with. Founder and owner of Pen Legacy®, Charron has been recognized as a literary game-changer who doesn't mind adapting words into legacies. She has authored 10 books, compiled 5 book anthologies, co-authored 2 books, published over 25 new authors, written, produced, and directed 1 short-film and 3 theatrical productions, contributed to more than 20 book anthologies, ghostwritten over 5 best-selling books, and been hired to adapt other novels into theatrical scripts. Just recently, she had the opportunity to produce and premiere her sold-out stage play, *Get Out of Your Own Way,* in Hollywood, California, and Times Square, New York.

Utilizing many of the same tactics commonly used today, Charron gave a new meaning to what it means to "share your truth" and exemplifies just how far your truth will take you. From her then-unprecedented writing techniques to the continuously innovative ways she uses social issues, current events, timeless messages, and her expertise on scriptwriting and storytelling, Charron remains a cutting-edge writer who pushes all boundaries.

Charron has a Bachelor of Arts in Political Science from West Chester University, a Master's in Public Administration from Keller Graduate School of Management, a Certificate in Paralegal Studies and Life Coaching, and a Doctorate of Philosophy (Humane Letters) from CICA International University & Seminary. She was also appointed as "Fellow of the Most Excellent Order of International Experts (FOIE)" in the field of Entrepreneurship from the United Nations and has been awarded and recognized for her work as an author and playwright.

Charron is a member of Zeta Phi Beta Sorority, Inc., Order of Eastern Star and First Baptist Church of Crestmont. She resides in Wesley Chapel, Florida, and is a proud mother of two sons, Christopher and Craig.

Also by Charron Monaye

BOOKS

My Side of the Story: From a Woman Waiting to Exhale

UnBreak My Heart: From Scorn to Finding Love Again

Love the Real You: Uncovering your "WHY" & Affirming You're Enough

STOP Asking for Permission & Give Notice: How to Accept & Attain Who You Are Without Validation

I Want to Quit My Job: 8 Entrepreneurial Strategies for Massive Results While Employed

Fear Is a Crime: How to Overcome Fear & Face Your Destiny

2018 Legacy Journal & Planner: A Planning Tool for Your Freedom & Future

I Matter Journal

Secure Your Legacy

When Shift Happens: 21 Days of Celebrating the Lessons of Life & Detours

CO-AUTHORED BOOKS

The Woodshed by: Jaguar Wright
The Shadow in My Eyes by: Deborah Rose

COMPILED ANTHOLOGIES

Bruised, Broken, and Blessed: Life Changing Stories That Will Ignite Hope, Elevate Personal Growth, and Confirm Your Greatness
Get Out of Your Own Way: Overcoming Adversity to Live in Your Truth Out Loud
Get Out of Your Own Way: 11 Life-Changing Stories on How to Face Everything & Rise!
Get Out of Your Own Way: 11 Game-Changing Stories on Mastering the Power of Trust, Faith & Success
Slay Your Legacy: 9 Keys to Manifesting the Life You Want

PLAYWRIGHT/PRODUCER

Living Your Life
Why Can't We Be Friends "An Anti-Bullying Production"
Til Death Do Us Part
Olivia Lost & Turned Out
Get Out of Your Own Way

PLAYWRIGHT/PRODUCER

Living Your Life
Why Can't We Be Friends "An Anti-Bullying Production"
Til Death Do Us Part
Olivia Lost & Turned Out
Get Out of Your Own Way

SCREENWRITER/ DIRECTOR/PRODUCER

A Childhood Lost

Recognition & Accolades

Office of the Hudson County Executive Citation, State of New Jersey

New Jersey General Assembly Resolution, Trenton, New Jersey

City of Jersey City Certificate of Recognition, Mayor Steven Fulop

The State of New Jersey Senate Citation, New Jersey Legislature

Doctorate of Philosophy (Humane Letters), CICA International University & Seminary.

Appointed as "Fellow of the Most Excellent Order of International Experts (FOIE)", The United Nations

Best Independent Author Award, Girls On Fire Awards

Presidential Award, Girls On Fire Awards

Award of Recognition in Entrepreneurship and Women Empowerment, Women Doing It Big Awards

Outstanding Contribution to Poetry, Great Poets Across America

www.ingramcontent.com/pod-product-compliance
Lightning Source LLC
Chambersburg PA
CBHW071357160426
42811CB00111B/2205/J